D0429582

Reach for the Stars™

Give up the good to go for the great.

Compiled by Dan Zadra
Designed by Kobi Yamada and Steve Potter

COM·PEN´·DI·UM™
Incorporated

ACKNOWLEDGEMENTS

These quotations were gathered lovingly but unscientifically over several years and/or contributed by many friends or acquaintances. Some arrived—and survived in our files—on scraps of paper and may therefore be imperfectly worded or attributed. To the authors, contributors and original sources, our thanks, and where appropriate, our apologies. —The Editors

WITH SPECIAL THANKS TO

Gerry Baird, Jay Baird, Justi Baumgardt, Neil Beaton, Rob & Beth Bingham, Doug Cruickshank, Jim Darragh, Josie & Rob Estes, Jennifer Hurwitz, Dick Kamm, Beth Keane, Liam Lavery, Connie McMartin, Jim & Teri O'Brien, Janet Potter & Family, Diane Roger, Sam Sundquist, Jenica Wilkie, Heidi Wills, Robert & Val Yamada, Tote Yamada, Anne Zadra, and August & Arline Zadra

CREDITS

Compiled by Dan Zadra
Designed by Kobi Yamada and Steve Potter

Printed in Hong Kong

GIVE UP THE GOOD TO GO FOR THE GREAT.

Reach for the Stars

"We have forty million reasons,
and not a single excuse."

—Rudyard Kipling

The greatest waste of our natural resources is the
number of people or companies that never achieve
their potential. Not only never achieve it, but don't
even try. Someone has a bright idea, and someone
else says it can't be done. Gather enough reasons
why it can't be done and, sure enough, it won't be
done. Won't even be attempted. Simple as that.

In the 1960's, John F. Kennedy said, "Let's put a
man on the moon in this decade." The immediate
fallout was predictable: "Can't be done...it's
unrealistic...not enough time...too many unanswered
questions." One mathematician estimated that 60
million separate decisions, operations and activities
would have to be coordinated in order to design,
create, launch and safely land a lunar expedition.
That's a pretty good reason not to try.

But they tried anyway. Armand Hammer once
wrote, "High intention sets the universe in motion."
He wasn't talking about God, he was talking about

you and me—about all the ordinary everyday people who pursue (or fail to pursue) their biggest dreams or brightest aspirations. Kennedy's lunar aspiration was so big and so exciting that it finally galvanized the worldwide scientific community, setting the necessary wheels in motion to achieve it.

How exciting are your dreams? Exciting enough to override all the reasons and excuses? We can help each other set the wheels in motion. We can say, "It will never fly"—or we can say, "We'll never know until we try." We can say, "It's never been done before"—or "We have the opportunity to be first." We can say, "We don't have the resources"—or "Let's be resourceful." We can say, "We don't have the expertise"—or "Let's network with those who do."

We only pass this way once. If you believe in something good, then give it a chance to happen. One day you'll realize that you not only reached for the stars, you grabbed a handful.

Dan Zadra

Believe it!
High expectations
are the key to
everything.

—Sam Walton

Your world is as big
as you make it.
—Georgia Douglas Johnson

We always underestimate
the future.
—Charles Kettering

Dream passionate dreams.
Design their reality.
—Candis Fancher

I am not a human being,
I am dynamite.

—Friedrich Nietzsche

Never be bullied
into silence. Never allow
yourself to be made a victim.
Accept no one's definition of
your life; define yourself.

—Harvey Fierstein

There is more here than
meets the eye.

—Lady Murasaki

I am not afraid....
I was born to do this.

—Joan of Arc

Seek and you will find.
Don't be willing to
accept an ordinary life.

—James and Salle Merrill Redfield

March to the beat
of your own drummer.

—Henry David Thoreau

Not all horses
were born equal.
A few were born to win.

—Mark Twain

There are incalculable
resources in the human spirit,
once it has been
set free.

—Hubert H. Humphrey

We are all capable
of everything.

—Virgil

Before you can win,
you have to believe
you are worthy.

—Mike Ditka

Every spirit builds itself
a house, and beyond its house
a world, and beyond its world
a heaven. Know then
that world exists for you.

—Ralph Waldo Emerson

Realize how good
you really are.

—Og Mandino

11

Never let the
fear of striking out
get in your way.

—Babe Ruth

Be careful what you
think and say. Life might
be listening and give you
less next time.

—Kobi Yamada

What you think,
you become.

—Mohandas Gandhi

The answers you get depend
upon the questions you ask.

—Thomas Kuhn

We are not passive spectators,
but active contestants in
the drama of our existence.
We need to take responsibility
for the kind of life we create
for ourselves.

—Nathaniel Branden, Ph.D.

If you know what you want,
you will recognize it when
you see it.

—Bill Cosby

This life is worth living,
we can say, since it is
what we make it.

—William James

Examine the labels you
apply to yourself. Every label is
a boundary or limit you will not
let yourself cross.

—Dwayne Dyer

Ain't gonna let nobody
turn me around....

—African-American spiritual

If your dream is big enough,
the facts don't count.

—Don Ward

I had ambition not only to
go farther than anyone had
ever been, but as far as it
was possible to go.

—Captain James Cook

Let's give the historians
something to write about.

—Propertius

Live your life while you have it.
Life is a splendid gift—there is
nothing small about it.

—Florence Nightingale

I dared to dream big dreams,
and then I willed them to happen.
I'm convinced that most people
can achieve their dreams and
beyond if they have the
determination to keep trying.

—Howard Schultz

Be so good
they can't ignore you.

—Jerry Dunn

Forsake all
inhibitions.
Pursue thy
dreams!

—Walt Whitman

All things are possible once
you make them so.

—Goethe

It's the possibility of
having a dream come true
that makes life interesting.

—Beth Bingham

Miracles happen to those
who believe in them.

—Bernard Berenson

18

Listen to your dreams—
those are the sounds
no one else can hear.

—Kobi Yamada

Some things have to be
believed to be seen.

—Ralph Hodgson

Faith is building on what
you know is here so you can
reach what you know is there.

—Cullen Hightower

I believe in the
power of dreams. I can be
anything, go anywhere.

—Des'ree

Open your arms
as wide as you can to
receive all the miracles
with your name on them.

—Sarah Ban Breathnach

Never fear the space
between your dreams and
reality. If you can dream it,
you can make it so.

—Belva Davis

When we stop dreaming,
we stop living.

—Lorrie Morgan

Not truth, but faith, is
what keeps the world alive.

—Edna St. Vincent Millay

Faith is not
complacent; faith is
action. You don't have
faith and wait. When you
have faith, you move.

—Betty Eadie

Doubt your doubts.

—Joe Batten

Our doubts are traitors
and make us lose the good
we oft might win by fearing
the attempt.

—Shakespeare

All we are given are
possibilities—to make ourselves
one thing or another.

—Jose Ortega y Gasset

Follow the tugs that
come from the heart.
I think that everyone gets
these gentle urges and should
listen to them. Even if they
sound absolutely insane, they
may be worth going with.

—Victoria Moran

You have a unique
message to deliver, a unique
song to sing, a unique act of
love to bestow. This message,
this song, and this act of love
have been entrusted exclusively
to the one and only you.

—John Powell, S.J.

The Promised Land
always lies on the other
side of the wilderness.

—Havelock Ellis

You'll see it
when you believe it.

—Denis Waitley

If what's in your dreams
wasn't already real inside you,
you couldn't even dream it.

—Gloria Steinem

Let me listen to me
and not to them.

—Gertrude Stein

If the people around you
don't believe in you, if they
don't encourage you, then
you need to find some
people who do.

—John Maxwell

A critic is someone who never
actually goes to the battle yet
who afterwards comes out
shooting the wounded.

—Tyne Daly

I am very aware that we can
only think one thought at
a time. So I refuse to think
the negative thoughts that
keep the good out.

—Louise L. Hay

They can conquer
who believe they can.

—Virgil

What I admire in Columbus
is not his having discovered a
world, but his having gone to
search for it on the faith
of an opinion.

—Turgot

Your vision will become
clear only when you can look
into your own heart.

—Carl Jung

There are better
things ahead than any
we leave behind.

—C.S. Lewis

No one has ever
seen tomorrow.

—Steven Fortere

Decide that
you want it
more than you
are afraid of it.

—Bill Cosby

You can't test
courage cautiously.

—Anne Dillard

We can scare ourselves or
inspire ourselves....We are
the architects of our own
attitudes and experiences.
We design the world by the
way we choose to see it.

—Barry Neil Kaufman

Drive out fear.

—Dr. W. Edwards Deming

No noble thing can be
done without risks.

—Michel Eyquem de Montaigne

The little things, I can obey.
But the big things—how we think,
what we value—those you must
choose yourself. You can't let
anyone—or society—determine
those for you.

—Morrie Schwartz

All serious daring
starts from within.

—Eudora Welty

The reason for the journey
is this: in a journey,
discoveries are made.

—Kobi Yamada

Lord, make me so
uncomfortable that I will
do the very thing I fear.

—Ruby Dee

The most important question
is: "Are you ready?"

—Johnny Carson

You cannot
discover new oceans
unless you have the courage
to lose sight of the shore.

—Daniel Abraham

"Come to the edge," he said.
They said, "We are afraid."
"Come to the edge," he said.
They came. He pushed
them...and they flew.

—Guillaume Apollinaire

Abolish fear and you can
accomplish anything you wish.

—Dr. C.E. Welch

Some experiences
simply do not translate.
You have to *go* to *know*.

—Kobi Yamada

Self-confidence is
the first requisite to
great undertakings.

—Samuel Johnson

Faith is...not being sure,
but betting with your
last cent.

—Mary Jean Irion

That which is
not daring is nothing.

—Kenneth Patchen

Until the day of his
death, no one can be
sure of his courage.

—Jean Anoulih

If you're not a player,
then you're just a passive
bystander—or worse,
a victim.

—Jon Kabat-Zinn, Ph.D.

The person who does not
make a choice makes a choice.

—Jewish proverb

It's a sad day when
you find out that it's not
accident or time or fortune
but just yourself that
kept things from you.

—Lillian Hellman

Courage comes and goes.
Hold on for the next supply.

—Thomas Merton

Guts get you there.

—B.C. Forbes

Safety is the most
unsafe path you can take,
safety keeps you numb and
dead. People are caught by
surprise when it is time
to die. They have allowed
themselves to live so little.

—Steven Levine

Those who fear life are
already three parts dead.

—Bertrand Russell

Living in fear is like
being frozen.

—Sharon Salzberg

Change doesn't happen
in the middle. It only happens
when we venture over to the
edge and take one small
step after another.

—Karen Sheridan

Remove failure as an option
and your chances for success
become infinitely better.

—Joan Lunden

There are some
decisions in life that
only you can make.

—Merle Shain

The greatest secret
of success in life is for a
person to be ready when
their opportunity comes.

—Benjamin Disraeli

We must dare, and dare again,
and go on daring.

—George Jacques Danton

You must
begin wherever
you are.

—Jack Boland

The future starts today,
not tomorrow.

—Virginia Satir

Don't let the
odds scare you from
even trying.

—Howard Schultz

You must
take your chance.

—William Shakespeare

Get started...and
keep going.

—Diane Roger

There is a time for
departure even when there's
no certain place to go.

Tennessee Williams

Do you seize
opportunities, or do you
let them slip by?

—John Gray, Ph.D.

All large tasks are completed
in a series of starts.

—Neil Fiore

Don't give up. Keep going.
There is always a chance
that you will stumble onto
something terrific. I have
never heard of anyone
stumbling over anything
while sitting down.

—Ann Landers

Be not afraid of going slowly,
be afraid of standing still.

—Chinese proverb

The days come and go,
but they say nothing, and if
we do not use the gifts they
bring, they carry them as
silently away.

—Ralph Waldo Emerson

Ain't no chance
if you don't take it.

—Guy Clark

To each of us, there come
opportunities to rearrange our
assumptions—not necessarily
to be rid of the old, but
more to profit from adding
something new.

—Leo Buscaglia

Great accomplishments
must be worked into being,
they cannot be worried
into being.

—Kobi Yamada

There are only two important
kinds of courage: the courage
to die and the courage to
get up in the morning.

—Jean Louis Servan-Schreiber

It is not enough to stare
up the steps, we must step
up the stairs.

—Vaclav Havel

What's courage but having
faith instead of fear?

—Michael J. Fox

The "what if" question
begs for completion:
"What if we tried...?"

—Dale Dauten

To know oneself,
one should assert oneself.

—Albert Camus

If nothing changes—
nothing changes.

—Jim Westley

No one can go back and
make a brand-new start,
my friend, but anyone can
start from here and make
a brand-new end.

—Dan Zadra

There are many wonderful
things that will never be done
if you do not do them.

—Honorable Charles D. Gill

What would life be if
we had no courage to
attempt anything?

—Vincent van Gogh

I will persist. I will always
take another step. If that is
of no avail I will take another,
and yet another.

—Og Mandino

Courage is only an
accumulation of small steps.

—George Konrad

Travelers, there is no path,
paths are made by walking.

—Antonio Machado

There's a big difference
between seeing an opportunity
and seizing an opportunity.

—Jim Moore

Very few people have
excellence thrust upon them.

—John Gardner

Life is a day-to-day,
moment-to-moment
experience.

—Salle Merrill Redfield

It doesn't matter what road
you take, hill you climb, or path
you're on, you will always end
up in the same place, learning.

—Ralph Stevenson

Fear not that life shall
come to an end, but rather
fear that it shall never
have a beginning.

—J.H. Newman

Everything
that is
was once
imagined.

—Ted Joans

People were born
to innovate, to invent.

—Microsoft

Imagination takes humility,
love and great courage.

—Carson McCullers

All life is
an experiment.

—Ralph Waldo Emerson

Creativity is
within everyone.

—Rene McPherson

Refuse to accept the many
reasons why it can't be done
and ask if there are any
reasons that it can be done.

—Hanoch McCarty

The difficulty lies
not so much in developing
new ideas as in escaping
from the old ones.

—John Maynard Keynes

The one who asks questions
doesn't lose his way.

—Akan proverb

A workable measure of
your progress is how fast
you can get free when
you are stuck and how many
ways you know to get free.

—Kathlyn Hendricks

What you focus
on increases.

—Rob Estes

If you believe it will work out...
you'll see opportunities.
If you believe it won't...
you'll see obstacles.

—Anonymous

People are always blaming
their circumstances for what
they are. I don't believe in
circumstances. The people
who get on in this world are
the people who get up and
look for the circumstances
they want, and if they can't
find them, make them.

—George Bernard Shaw

Nothing can stop the one with the right mental attitude from achieving the goal; nothing on earth can help the one with the wrong mental attitude.

—Brian Lee

On the other side of nothing is everything.

—Martin Spears

The illiterates of the future are not those who cannot read or write. They are those who cannot learn, unlearn, and relearn.

—Alvin Toffler

Anything can happen.
That's the beauty of creating.

—Ernie Harwell

Imagination is the
beginning of creation.
We imagine what we desire;
we will what we imagine; and at
last we create what we will.

—George Bernard Shaw

A rock pile ceases to be a rock
pile the moment a single man
contemplates it, bearing within
him the image of a cathedral.

—Antoine de Saint-Exupery

Assumptions are the
death of possibilities.

—James Mapes

To invent, you need a goal,
imagination and a pile of junk.

—Thomas Edison

The first rule of
intelligent tinkering is to
save all the parts.

—Aldo Leopold

The next time your
mind wanders, follow it
around for awhile.

—Jessica Masterson

Originality is not doing
something no one else has
ever done, but doing what has
been done countless times
with new life, new breath.

—Marie Chapian

I start where the
last person left off.

—Thomas Edison

You can't see the
good ideas behind you
by looking twice as hard as
what's in front of you.

—Roger von Oech

Every life has
its share of setbacks and
disappointments—of tragedy
and loss. How do we keep our
inner fire alive? Two things,
at minimum, are needed:
an ability to appreciate the
positives in our life—and
a commitment to action.

—Nathaniel Branden, Ph.D.

If you are on a road to nowhere, find another road.

—Ashanti proverb

When you know what you want and you want it badly enough, you can always find ways to get it.

—Jim Rohn

Instead of wallowing in my misery, I just made some changes.

—Stephanie Mills

Hurdles are in your life for jumping.

—Rev. Sharon Poindexter

He knows not
his own strength that
hath not met adversity.

—Ben Johnson

Only those who
dare to fail greatly can
ever achieve greatly.

—Robert F. Kennedy

Paralyze resistance
with persistence.

—Frank Tyger

Doubt is often the
beginning of wisdom.

—Dr. M. Scott Peck

Most successes have been
built on failures; not on one
failure alone, but on several.
The majority of the great
historic accomplishments
have been the final result of
a persistent struggle against
discouragement and failure.

—Charles Gow

Change is not made
without inconvenience,
even from worse to better.

—Richard Hooker

Sometimes the best
credential is scar tissue
formed by battling resistance
to a great idea.

—Dan Zadra

When we dim our light,
we invite mediocrity.

—Kris King

Why do people give up big
dreams for small realities?

—Kevin Costner

When we do face the
difficult times, we need to
remember that circumstances
don't make a person, they
reveal a person.

—Richard Carlson, Ph.D.

I had gotten to the point
where I was either going to
play the violin much better or
I was going to break it
over my knee.

—Ellen Taaffe Zwilich

So much of our journey
is learning about and
removing barriers.

—Melody Beattie

I merely took the
energy it takes to pout
and wrote some blues.

—Duke Ellington

We have the ability to face
adversity—to come from
behind and win with grace.

—Amber Brookman

When we can
no longer change a
situation, we are challenged
to change ourselves.

—Victor Frankl

Every adversity, every
failure, and every heartbreak
carries with it the seed of an
equivalent or greater benefit.

—Napoleon Hill

You can only go halfway into
the darkest forest, then you
are coming out the other side.

—Chinese proverb

I ate today,
and I was not eaten.

—Robert Fulghum

You have to accept whatever
comes and the only important
thing is that you meet it
with courage and with the
best you have to give.

—Eleanor Roosevelt

We take on the strength
of that which we overcome.

—Guy M. Lewis

I loathe the idea of
being powerless.

—Mary Beth Edelson

Obstacles don't have to stop you.
If you run into a wall, don't turn
around and give up. Figure out
how to climb it, go through it,
or work around it.

—Michael Jordan

Even the darkest hour
has only sixty minutes.

—Morris Mandel

You failed many times,
although you may not
remember. You fell down
the first time you tried
to walk. You almost drowned
the first time you tried to
swim, didn't you? Did you
hit the ball the first time
you swung a bat?

—United Technologies

Do not turn back when
you are just at the goal.

—Publilius Syrus

A delay is not a denial.

—Rev. James Cleveland

If you fall,
fall on your back.
If you can look up,
you can get up.

—Les Brown

You cannot fix
what you will not face.

—James Baldwin

You can't
build the
future in
the future.

—Charles Gedding

We vote with our actions.

—Benjamin Shield

Go on working,
freely and furiously, and
you will make progress.

—Paul Gauguin

We must travel in the
direction of our fear.

—John Berryman

Faith helps you succeed
when everything else fails.

—Dawn Ewing

Change what you can,
accept what you can't.

—Joan Lunden

Faith steers us
through stormy seas,
moves mountains and
jumps across oceans.

—Mahatma Gandhi

I do not admire giving up.

—Janet Burrowa

It takes a deep commitment
to change and an even
deeper commitment to grow.

—Ralph Ellison

If winter comes,
can spring be far behind?

—Percy Bysshe Shelley

Faith without work
cannot be called faith.

—Mitchell Smyte

You must learn how to make it
on the broken pieces.

—Rev. Louise Williams-Bishop

Take charge
of your thoughts.

—Plato

If you want to moan, complain, or focus on your problems, it's okay with me. But I have a two-for-one rule: For every minute we spend on complaints, we have to spend two on solutions to the problem. If I have 30 minutes to spend with you, 10 can be spent listening to your problems and then you've got to promise to spend 20 on figuring out what to do about them.

—Margie Ingram

What you give, you get—
ten times over.

—Yoruba proverb

When I was just getting
started, someone told me,
if you make ten calls a day
you are bound to get work.
I made twenty.

—Sam Grey

Work will always win
what wishing won't.

—Michael Nolan

Care enough for a result,
and you will almost
certainly attain it.

—William James

No victor believes in chance.

—Nietzsche

Our greatest weakness lies
in giving up. The certain way to
succeed is always to try just
one more time.

—Thomas Edison

The real moment of success is not the moment apparent to the crowd.

—George Bernard Shaw

Be proud of how far you have come—and have faith in how far you can go!

—Richard Springs

What difference does it make if the thing you're scared of is real or not?

—Toni Morrison

There is a reason for
all things. Faith means
we don't always have to
have the answer.

—Petey Parker

Faith in small things has
repercussions that ripple all
the way out. In a huge,
dark room a little match
can light up the place.

—Joni Eareckson Tada

Don't let your fear grow
bigger than your faith.

—Josie Bissett

Somewhere on the
great world the sun is
always shining, and it will
sometimes shine on you.

—Myrtle Reed

It's a good life if you
don't weaken.

—Richard Carlson, Ph.D.

Interest in the changing
seasons is a much happier
state of mind than being
hopelessly in love with spring.

—George Santayana

Faith is daring to go farther
than you can see.

—William Newton Clarke

When you come to the edge of
all the light you have, and must
take a step into the darkness
of the unknown, believe that
one of two things will happen.
Either there will be something
solid for you to stand on—
or you will be taught how to fly.

—Patrick Overton

There isn't a person anywhere
who isn't capable of doing more
than he thinks he can.

—Henry Ford

It is always too soon to quit.

—Gil Atkinson

The place where you lose
your path is not necessarily
where it ends.

—Kobi Yamada

May I never miss a sunset
or a rainbow because
I am looking down.

—Sara June Parker

Working together works!

—Dr. Rob Gilbert

None of us can go it alone.
Support your team.

—Dr. Robert Schuller

Leave no one out of the
big picture. Involve everyone in
everything of any consequence
to all of you.

—Tom Peters

Absolute individualism is
an absurdity.

—Henri-Frederic Amiel

The purpose of freedom
is to create it for others.

—Bernard Malamud

Don't be fooled
into thinking you are
alone on your journey.
You're not. Your struggle
is everyone's struggle.
Your pain is everyone's pain.
Your power is everyone's
power. It is simply that we take
different paths along
our collective journey.

—Benjamin Shield, Ph.D.

If you and I exchange a
dollar, we still have only
one dollar a piece. But, if we
exchange ideas, you have two
ideas and I have two ideas.

—Dan Zadra

I believe in the essential
unity of all that lives.
Therefore, I believe that if
one person gains spiritually,
the whole world gains,
and that if one person falls,
the whole world falls
to that extent.

—Mahatma Gandhi

The older I get, the more convinced I am of the direct correlation between our success with relationships and virtually everything of significance in life.

—Glenn Van Ekeren

Success is empty if you arrive at the finish line alone. The best reward is to get there surrounded by winners. The more winners you can bring with you—the more gratifying the victory.

—Howard Schultz

Making a consistent small
investment in people can
reproduce itself to create
an outstanding return.

—Scott Johnson

Never lose sight
of the fact that the most
important yardstick of your
success will be how you treat
other people—your family,
friends, and co-workers,
and even strangers you
meet along the way.

—Barbara Bush

It is good to let a little
sunshine out as well as in.

—Mary Heider

Those who believe in
our ability do more than
stimulate us. They create
for us an atmosphere in which
it becomes easier to succeed.

—John H. Spalding

I don't think God cares
where we graduated or what
we did for a living. God wants
to know who we are.

—Bernie Siegel, M.D.

We don't try to be
100 percent better;
rather one percent better
in 100 ways.

—Ann Mitchell

Help others get ahead.
You always stand taller
with someone else on
your shoulders.

—Bob Moawad

I believe you can have everything
you want out of life if you just
help enough other people get
what they want out of life.

—Zig Ziglar

Integrity
has no need
of rules.

—Albert Camus

Integrity is a constant
companion on the extra mile.

—Kelly Williams

Courage is not simply
one of the virtues, but
the form of every virtue
at the testing point.

—C.S. Lewis

There are no shortcuts to
anyplace worth going.

—Beverly Sills

It does not require many
words to speak the truth.

—Chief Joseph

If I can relate to
this moment with integrity,
and then this moment with
integrity, and then this
moment with integrity, then
the sum of that is going to
be great over a lifetime.

—Jon Kabat-Zinn, Ph.D.

Fewness of words,
greatness of deeds.

—Abdul Baha

Life is too long
not to do it right.

—Diane Deacon

Hold yourself to a higher
standard than anybody else
expects of you.

—Henry Ward Beecher

What is the quality
of your intent?

—Thurgood Marshall

People are all alike
in their promises. It is
only in their deeds that
they are different.

—Jean Baptiste Moliere

The difference between
right and almost right is the
difference between lightning
and the lightning bug.

—Mark Twain

The truth is more important
than the facts.

—Frank Lloyd Wright

I am for integrity,
if only because life is
very short and truth
is hard to come by.

—Kermit Eby

The willingness to accept
responsibility for one's own
life is the source from which
self-respect springs.

—Joan Didion

Courage makes it possible to
do the right thing when the
right thing is unpopular.

—David Wecker

Find your true path.
It's so easy to become
someone we don't want to be,
without even realizing it's
happening. We are created by
the choices we make every day.

—Bernie Siegel, M.D.

I don't know who my
grandfather was; I am
more concerned about what
his grandson will be.

—Abraham Lincoln

By the work
one knows the worker.

—Jean De La Fontaine

If you do your best,
what else is there?

—Gen. George Patton

I focus day after day
principally on what I care
most about in this world—
on what I most respect and
admire. That is what I give
my time and attention to.

—Nathaniel Branden, Ph.D.

As long as the day lasts,
let's give it all we've got.

—David O. McKay

If you are not totally free,
ask yourself, why?

—Stuart Wilde

If you don't like what you're
getting back in life, take a look
at what you're putting out.

—Pamela Dreyer

One of life's most
painful moments comes
when we must admit that
we didn't do our homework,
that we are not prepared.

—Merlin Olsen

Great works do not
always lie in our way,
but every moment we may
do little ones excellently,
that is, with great love.

—Francis De Sales

You don't need to have victims
to have a victory.

—Dan Zadra

A good head and
a good heart are always a
formidable combination.

—Nelson Mandela

We grow a little every
time we do not take advantage
of somebody's weakness.

—Bern Williams

You don't have to blow
out the other person's light
to let your own shine.

—Bernard M. Baruch

Count no day lost in which
you waited your turn, took
only your share and sought
advantage over no one.

—Robert Brault

Happiness is always a
by-product. You don't make
yourself happy by chasing
happiness. You make yourself
happy by being a good person.

—Unknown

When I am working on
a problem, I never think
about beauty. I think about
how to solve the problem.
But when I've finished, if the
solution isn't beautiful,
I know it's wrong.

—Buckminster Fuller

Compared to what we might be, we are only half awake.

—William James

We are all capable of much
more than we think we are.

—Lao Tzu

Be faithful to that which
exists nowhere but in yourself.

—Andre Gide

I don't want to represent
humanity as it is, but only
as it might be.

—Albert Camus

I am my own heroine.

—Marie Bashkirtseff

Your crown has been
bought and paid for.
All you must do is
put it on your head.

—James Baldwin

Give me a place to stand
and I can move the world.

—Archimedes

God always knew
I had it in me and finally
convinced me, too.

—Iyanla Vanzant

We all wish you happiness
and we will support you,
help you, cheer for you.
But our wishes cannot give
you success. It can only
come from yourself,
from the spirit within you.

—Rev. W. Ralph Ward, Jr.

Our prayers are answered
not when we are given
what we ask, but when
we are challenged to be
what we can be.

—Morris Adler

I was lucky to be
brought up loved. Not that
everything I did was liked, but
I knew that I was loved—
and knowing this gave me
the ability and freedom to be
who I wanted to be.

—Bernie Siegel, M.D.

Everyone has in them
something precious that
is in no one else.

—Martin Buber

If you are David, why
aren't you fully David?
If you are Susan, why aren't
you completely Susan?
We are here on earth to
become who we are
meant to be.

—Angeles Arrien

If you are willing, great things
are possible to you.

—Grenville Kleiser

Every day in every way
I'm getting better and better.

—Emile Coue

When you believe in something,
and you carry it in your heart,
you accept no excuses,
only results.

—Ken Blanchard

What I have now, I know
that no army can take
from me. I have myself.

—Michael J. Fox

The greatest thing is
to be willing to give up who
we are in order to become
all that we can become.

—Max De Pree

When we don't enjoy what
we do, we only nick the
surface of our potential.

—Dennis Wholey

Where your pleasure is,
there is your treasure;
where your treasure, there
your heart; where your heart,
there your happiness.

—Augustine

It is only in the heart that
anything really happens.

—Ellen Glasgow

For all of us, the key is to pay
close attention to which activities
make us feel most alive and in
love with life—and then try to
spend as much time as possible
engaged in those activities.

—Nathaniel Branden, Ph.D

You must find the passion,
an unrelenting passion.

—David Easton

Experience teaches us
in a millennium what passion
teaches us in an hour.

—Ralph Iron

The heart has eyes the
brain knows nothing of.

—Charles Parkhurst

Nothing great
was ever created
without enthusiasm.

—Ralph Waldo Emerson

The pitcher cries out
for water to carry, and
a person cries out for
work that is real.

—Marge Piercy

I feel that the greatest
reward for doing is the
opportunity to do more.

—Jonas Salk

Not to go out
and do your best is
to sacrifice the gift.

—Steve Prefontaine

You must give your own story to the world.

—Carter G. Woodsen

Realize that life is
the best thing ever, and
that you have no business
taking it for granted.

—Anna Quindlen

We have a limited
number of heartbeats
and we're in charge of
how we use them.

—Peter Alsop

Never let an
adventure pass you by.

—Joan Lunden

It is not length of life,
but depth of life.

—Ralph Waldo Emerson

We all live in suspense,
from day-to-day, from
hour-to-hour; in other
words, we are the hero
of our own story.

—Mary McCarthy

Be glad you
had the moment.

—Steve Shagan

May you grow to be
as beautiful as God
meant you to be when
He first thought of you.

—Elizabeth Trent

Destiny leaves itself like a
trail of bread crumbs, and
by the time you have found
your way to the maker of the
tracks, it's inside of you,
a part of you forever.

—Kobi Yamada

There is a dream dreaming us.

—A Kalahari Bushman

Real generosity toward
the future consists in giving
all to what is present.

—Albert Camus

Imagine what a harmonious
world it could be if every
single person, both young
and old, shares a little of what
he or she is good at doing.

—Quincy Jones

Follow what you love and
it will take you where
you want to go.

—Natalie Goldberg

The greatest thing
in the world is to know
how to be oneself.

—Montaigne

It's about following
your bliss, losing it,
and finding it again.

—Natalie Chapman

We find what we
search for—or, if we don't
find it, we become it.

—Jessamyn West

Take the time to
listen to your heart.

—Jack Kornfield

If we fail to nourish our souls,
they wither, and without soul,
life ceases to have meaning.

—Marion Woodman, Ph.D.

Learn what you are
and be such.

—Pindar

How far you go in life
depends on your being tender
with the young, compassionate
with the aged, sympathetic
with the striving, and tolerant
of the weak and strong,
because someday in your life,
you will have been all of these.

—George Washington Carver

There is no feeling
in a human heart which
exists in that heart alone—
which is not, in some form
or degree, in every heart.

—George MacDonald

Love everybody you love;
you can never tell when they
might not be there.

—Nancy Bush Ellis

It is the experience of
living that is important,
not searching for meaning.
We bring meaning by
how we love the world.

—Bernie Siegel, M.D.

People carry around
an enormous amount of
grief because they missed
the little things.

—Jon Kabat-Zinn, Ph.D.

The highest reward for a
person's work is not what
they get for it, but what
they become by it.

—John Ruskin

Success depends on
the degree to which you
are at peace with yourself.
If you have people around
you who love you, and you
have peace with what
you're doing, it doesn't get
any better than that.

—Og Mandino

The blessings for which we hunger are not to be found in other places or people. These gifts can only be given to you by yourself.

—John O'Donohue

Love is all that truly matters and is the only real measure of our success as human beings.

—Richard Carlson, Ph.D.

No one can give us wisdom. We must discover it for ourselves, on the journey through life, which no one can take for us.

—Sun Bear

The aim,
if reached
or not,
makes great
the life.

—Robert Browning

Also available from Compendium Publishing are these spirited and compelling companion books of great quotations.

Be Happy.
Remember to live, love,
laugh and learn.

Because of You™
Celebrating the Difference
You Make™

Brilliance™
Uncommon Voices From
Uncommon Women™

Forever Remembered™
A Gift for the Grieving Heart.™

I Believe in You™
To your heart, your dream
and the difference you make.

Little Miracles™
To renew your dreams,
lift your spirits, and strengthen
your resolve.™

Thank You
In appreciation of you,
and all that you do

Together We Can™
Celebrating the power of
a team and a dream™

To Your Success™
Thoughts to Give Wings
to Your Work and Your
Dreams™

Whatever It Takes™
A Journey into the Heart
of Human Achievement™

You've Got a Friend™
Thoughts to Celebrate
the Joy of Friendship™

These books may be ordered directly from the publisher (800) 914-3327.
But please try your bookstore first!

www.compendiuminc.com